D1133886

CONTENTS

INTRODUCTION

The Pegan diet is a unique and relatively new style of eating, inspired by two of the most popular and very known diet trends: paleo and vegan diet. The Pegan diet incorporates essential advantages of both, taking their key components and concepts into account. As a result, it is claimed to be healthier than both of those diets. Don't be fooled by its name though, this is not a vegan diet and there are good reasons for that, which will be discussed further on.

To summarize, paleo eaters attempt to consume foods that were available around 2.6 million years ago, during the Paleolithic era, such as vegetables, fruits, nuts, meat and fish. Paleo eaters exclude from their diet processed foods, salt and sugar, grains and legumes, dairy oils, salt, and of course: coffee and alcohol.

Vegans, on the other hand, eat only plant-based meals and avoid consuming any animal products, including byproducts, such as meat, fish, eggs, dairy products, or honey. They, unlike paleo eaters, eat grains, beans and other legumes, along with plant-based fats and oils.

The Pegan diet enhances total bodily health by lowering inflammation, controlling blood sugar, and supplying your body with plenty of energy. This can be accomplished by consuming a lot of fresh vegetables, fruits, and whole foods on the one hand while limiting consumption of meat, fish and dairy products on the other. Pegan diet is not intended for short-term weight loss but rather as a way of life and everyday eating. Every year, more and more people decide to try it out because of its health benefits.

If you enjoy eating a variety of fruits and vegetables but occasionally crave for meat or fish as well, this may be the diet for you!

BENEFITS AND DOWNSIDES

The Pegan diet emphasizes healthy, wholesome meals that are high in vitamins and minerals that your body needs and can benefit your health in a variety of ways. It is also quite basic and straightforward. Unlike other dietary patterns, there is no need to measure proteins, carbohydrates, or calories, which makes long-term tracking easy.

Depending on your existing diet, practicing the Pegan diet can result in significant weight loss because you will eliminate unhealthy, starchy, and sugary foods from your diet. In addition to weight loss, the diet emphasizes healthful foods that can assist improve a variety of other areas of health.

The Pegan diet is primarily composed of fruits and vegetables, which are high in nutrients, such as fiber, minerals, and vitamins. This will provide your body with energy, enhance your immune system, and improve the appearance of your skin and hair.

The Pegan diet also encourages you to eat healthy fat, which is found in fish, nuts, seeds, and other plant-based foods, while discouraging you from eating bad fat and processed foods. High cholesterol, chronic inflammation, and heart disease can all be caused by eating bad fat (omega-6 fatty acids). Eating healthy fat (omega-3 fatty acids), on the other hand, has no negative impact on your body and is even beneficial as it increases the healthy cholesterol levels in your blood and helps with the absorption of vitamins A, K and other fat-soluble vitamins.

By avoiding processed foods, you will ensure that your body does not acquire any artificial colorings, flavorings, preservatives, or other ingredients, as well as too much sugar or salt, all of which can be damaging to your health.

If you are practicing the Pegan diet correctly and follow the rules, the diet is safe and associated with almost no negative side effects. However, you should be aware of the following concerns.

The first and most important concern is always your current health condition. If you have any underlying medical concerns, you should discuss them with your physician or dietitian before making any significant changes to your existing diet.

This diet may cause some difficulties for vegans or vegetarians since it also includes animal products. Pegan diet restricts the number of wholegrains and legumes ingested each day, which is the foundation of a plant-based diet. Meat, on the other hand, provides minerals such as iron, vitamin B12, calcium, iron, and potassium which are harder to obtain on a vegan diet. Following only a vegan version of the Pegan diet might be difficult and you should be sure to get enough protein and other nutrients on a daily basis. It is strongly advised that you adhere to all Pegan diet principles, not just the vegan portion of it.

The Pegan diet may be difficult for meat-eaters as well. They can easily eat too much of it due to the lack of other food groups. A high-protein, low-carbohydrate diet may, if practiced over long periods of time, cause kidney problems and osteoporosis for some people.

It is furthermore important to stress out that the Pegan diet prohibits you from eating a variety of foods that would otherwise be deemed nutritious and beneficial for you. Legumes, for example, are high in protein, fiber, and minerals like iron, zinc, and copper. The same is true for wholegrains, which are a highly nutritious source that can aid in the prevention of many chronic health disorders. For example, animal milk can provide your body with minerals such as calcium, vitamin D, protein, and potassium. However, it is generally avoided on the Pegan diet. Some experts, therefore, advise pegans to ingest a small amount of otherwise restricted foods and food categories on occasion, just to reach a fair balance among all food groups.

This diet also highlights lots of fresh ingredients and sustainably sourced animal products. While these foods are surely better for your health in the long run, they are usually more expensive and might impact your wallet.

Having said that, if you follow the diet and its rules correctly, plan your meals ahead of time, and consume enough high-quality and diverse food, you should be alright. After a period of time on the Pegan diet, you will feel lighter and more energetic, your skin and hair will glow owing to an abundance of vitamins and minerals, you will lose weight, and your entire physical health will improve.

PEGAN DIET MENU

FOODS TO EAT

Fruit and vegetables

A pegan diet gives you a lot of vitamins, minerals, fiber and energy. This is why fruit and vegetables should compose around 75% of the Pegan diet menu. Try to ensure that it is placed on every plate of food you eat. It should covert approx. ¾ or ⅔ of space on your plate. The fruit you are encouraged to eat should have a low glycemic index (GI), and the vegetables should be low in starch.

There are a few facts you should know about the GI. GI was developed by two physicians from the University of Toronto. GI assesses how rapidly carbs boost blood glucose levels and thus grades them on a scale of 0-100. The glycemic load (GL) was later developed by researchers to quantify digestible carbohydrates and their impact on blood sugar levels. The GL is computed by multiplying the grams of carbs in food by its GI number, then dividing by 100. Low GI carbohydrates are digested, absorbed, and metabolized more slowly. This leads to a lower increase in blood glucose levels, which would otherwise encourage fat storage. Stabilized blood sugar levels have been shown in studies to provide a variety of benefits, including sustained weight loss, reduced belly fat, and so on. A GI of less than 55 is considered low, 55-70 is considered medium, and 70 and beyond is considered high. A GL of 10 or less is regarded low, 11-19 is considered medium, and 20 or more is considered high.

Keeping blood sugar levels stabilized is one of the goals of the Pegan diet. That is why low GI fruit is advised. The following types of food with a low GI are recommended to eat:

- Peaches;
- Cherries;
- Fresh figs;
- Grapefruits;

- Strawberries;
- Raspberries;
- Oranges;
- Plums;
- Apples (especially green ones);
- Pears, etc.

Vegetables you are encouraged to eat should contain as little starch as possible, for example:

- Asparagus;
- Artichokes;
- Broccoli;
- Tomato;
- Cabbage;
- Cauliflower;
- Cucumber;
- Mushrooms;
- Spinach;
- Zucchini;
- Celery;
- Eggplant, etc.

All vegetables include starch, which is a type of complex carbohydrate. Starchy vegetables, as the name implies, contain more starch than others. This indicates they have a higher GI, which causes blood sugar levels to rise faster than foods with a lower glycemic index. For the same reasons, you should avoid fruit with a high GI. You should therefor also avoid starchy vegetables.

Protein

Protein should account for roughly 25% of the diet. Plant sources of protein include nuts, seeds, and legumes. You should prioritize those first.

Despite the fact that the Pegan diet is influenced by veganism, in which animal products are fully eschewed, you should not be misled because it's not a vegan nor a vegetarian diet.

There are grounds for not removing animal items from this diet. Vegans sometimes fight to achieve sufficient iron and protein levels. These nutrients are particularly vital as the body is becoming older and losing muscular mass. Animal protein sources also contain a lot of iron, zinc, phosphorus, and potassium, which are difficult to obtain on a vegan diet. Moreover, vitamin B12 is only naturally contained in beef and cannot be found in any other food items. Vegans that forgo those goods may require chemically produced vitamins to add to them, which may not be sufficient in the long run. Small quantities of meat, fish and eggs on the Pegan diet are therefore permitted.

Pegan diet thus allows you to eat small amounts of meat, fish and eggs. The amount of animal protein consumed is higher than in the vegan diet but substantially lower than in the paleo diet, where meat can account for up to 50% (or more) of your daily calorie intake.

It should be noted that animal protein should be used to supplement your residual protein demands that cannot be met by plant sources rather than as your primary protein source. Choose free-range animal products such as grass-fed beef, free-range poultry, and whole eggs.

Plant-based milk, such as flax milk, walnut milk, almond milk, soy milk, and coconut milk, as well as vegan types of yogurts, are among the healthier dairy alternatives and are a great substitute for an animal sourced diary.

As regards fish and other seafood, always go for a low-mercury option, for example: salmon, sardines, crabs, pollocks, squids, tilapia, trout, and anchovies. As a general rule, bigger fish with high mercury levels, such as shark, some types of tuna, swordfish and marlin, should be avoided. Mercury is found in trace levels in all types of fish, as they acquire mercury from their dietary sources. Smaller levels of mercury, usually found in smaller fish, do not represent a health risk for the majority of people. Mercury is naturally excreted from your body, but it can take months for it to do so. Mercury levels in adults can progressively rise, depending on what we eat, and eventually becoming detrimental to health. If consumed in larger amounts, mercury is harmful and poisonous as it may permanently damage our central nervous system, including our brain and spinal cord and damage our kidneys. It can also harm a developing fetus or a newborn child, so pregnant women should take extra precautions while consuming fish.

To avoid potential health hazards, stick with low mercury fish and seafood.

Legumes

Legumes and grains are beneficial to your body, according to the principles of the Pegan diet. However, legumes should not be consumed in high numbers, as they could be considered as starchy food sources and therefore, impact the sugar levels in your blood.

Consumption of gluten-free grains such as brown or black rice, quinoa, oats, millet, and amaranth is permitted but should be limited to less than half a cup every meal.

Fat

The Pegan diet, in general, promotes the consumption of fat. In fact, you may get about 25-35 percent of your daily calorie intake from fat, but it must come from the correct sources. Otherwise, it may compromise your health.

Healthy fat, high in omega-3 fatty acids, can be found in foods such as almonds, olives, and avocados. While on the Pegan diet, you can consume a large number of almonds, pistachios, walnuts, and other nuts. Peanuts should be avoided because they are considered a legume. You can use unrefined coconut oil or cold press olive or avocado oil to grease the pan on occasion.

You can also obtain fat from meat and fish, although as previously indicated, meat should be consumed in limited amounts and should come from a free-range animal and fish should be low in mercury.

On the other hand, you must avoid sources of harmful fat. For instance, processed food is usually covered in highly refined sunflower or canola oil and includes other unhealthy fat sources, such as margarine. Such foods contain omega 6 fatty acids, which are not healthy. The consumption of larger quantities of unhealthy fat over long periods of time usually causes chronic inflammation as well as high cholesterol levels. This impacts your weight, but more importantly and your heart, veins and liver health. This is why it is important to stick with healthy fat sources rich in omega-3 fatty acids, regardless of which type of diet you are practicing.

FOODS TO AVOID

The Pegan diet is more adaptable than the paleo or vegan diets since it allows for the occasional consumption of almost any food. Several foods and food groups, however, are strictly discouraged. Some of these foods are known to be unhealthy, while others, depending on who you ask, may be deemed highly healthy. The majority of these items are avoided because of their alleged impact on blood sugar and/or inflammation in the body.

In general, everything that comes out of a box, a glass jar, a can, a bakery paper bag, or anything else that our forefathers did not eat should be avoided.

More specifically, the Pegan diet often avoids the following sorts of food:

- Diary: avoid dairy items such as cow's milk, yogurt, and cheese. Foods derived from sheep or goat milk, on the other hand, are permitted in limited quantities. Butter derived from grass-fed cow's milk is also permitted in limited amounts because it is high in omega-3 fatty acids and hence very nutritious for your body.
- Fermented goods: fermented products should be avoided because they might cause inflammation.
- Fruits with a high GI, such as ripe mango, pineapple, black grapes, watermelon, and dates, are discouraged. However, you do not have to fully avoid it; in rare instances, you can consume it if not too ripe.
- Starch: Beans, potatoes, chickpeas, corn, lentils, parsnips, peas, sweet potatoes, yams, and other starchy veggies. Similar to fruits

with a high glycemic index, you can enjoy starchy veggies on rare occasions.

- Gluten: avoid all gluten-containing grains (wheat and other similar grains). Gluten-containing foods elevate fat levels in the body and induce weight gain, which is extremely hazardous. As a result, avoiding whole-grain bread, cereals, pasta, brown rice, and other high-fiber foods will help you stay healthy.
- Gluten-free grains: While even gluten-free grains are discouraged, moderate portions of gluten-free wholegrains are acceptable on occasion.
- Legumes: Most legumes are avoided because they have the potential to raise blood sugar levels. Low-starch legumes (such as lentils, mung beans, black beans, and so on) are acceptable.
- Salt and sugar: any added sugar (or salt), refined or not, should be avoided, but minimal amounts may still be used from time to time. Sugar can lead to addiction over time; moreover, eating sugary meals causes cravings throughout the day and can lead to weight gain, binge eating, low energy levels, constipation, and bad skin. It has also been connected to a number of heart disorders. Eating too much salt, on the other hand, can result in water retention, an increase in blood pressure, an increased risk of stomach cancer and heart disease, and so on.
- Refined oils: vegetable oils such as canola, soybean and sunflower oil are not allowed. They are heavily processed and include a lot of bad fat (omega-6 fatty acids), which is bad for your heart, cholesterol levels, and inflammation.
- Food additives: avoid artificial colorings, flavorings, preservatives, and other additions.
- Processed food: no industrially processed foods, such as chips, crackers, biscuits, granola, fast food, etc., are allowed. Certainly, avoiding processed foods entirely is critical for enhancing health and well-being, as there is just too much of it on the plate these days.

TIPS AND TRICKS

The Pegan diet is for the long haul. In a shorter period of time, you will not see much of a difference in terms of health benefits. It will take some time for your body to adjust and produce the desired benefits. So be patient, keep up the excellent effort, and never give up hope. It will occur.

Try preparing your own meals; it will help you better understand your body. Making food for oneself also ensures that you've been eating clean recently because it's all in front of your eyes.

In addition, the ratio of 75 percent fruits and vegetables to 25 percent protein may be too much for you. This is especially true if you are a beginner and are only just getting started with this type of diet. If the ratio appears to be unachievable, attempt to use it as a general guideline. Perhaps you might strive to achieve this target on a daily or weekly basis, rather than inside each particular meal. It will become easier over time as your body adjusts to your new food plan.

You must dedicate a significant amount of time to meal planning and preparation in order to practice the Pegan diet. It is easier if you have some cooking experience. This is due to the restriction of some food groups, as well as the avoidance of processed foods, which makes preparing a daily meal difficult and stressful.

The Pegan diet also contains a variety of items that are often more expensive. Thus this diet may have a considerable financial impact on yourself. Cow milk, for example, is typically less expensive than plant-based milk, and margarine is less expensive than olive or avocado oil. Gluten-free items are significantly more expensive than gluten-containing products. It is therefore not a crime if you opt for items, which include gluten, especially if you are not allergic to it, or cow milk, to help your wallet out.

Also, keep in mind that it is best to gradually adjust your present diet, especially if you are a newbie. If you are not in a hurry to lose weight, you can begin the pegan lifestyle by eating more and more like a pegan on a daily basis. Instead of rushing into a drastic shift in your everyday diet, you can gradually prepare your body for it. Don't feel awful if you cheat on your diet from time to time. Most crucial, do not eliminate something you enjoy eating. This generally backfires and can throw you off track. Try to have fun and be creative on your adventure!

Cravings may test you at times, but you should manage your desires and adhere to your strategy. Replacing some foods with healthier alternatives, such as switching from ordinary milk to goat milk, which is easier to digest, or choosing coconut yogurt or vegan cheese, will alleviate many of your problems.

On the following pages, you will get to know delicious recipe ideas, along with a 2-week diet plan that will help you get your pegan lifestyle started. Let's not waste any more time. Dig into it and enjoy!

BREAKFAST

Deviled Eggs

Prep time: 5 min	Cook time: 10 min	Servings: 6

Ingredients

- 6 large eggs, hard-boiled
- ¼ cup avocado mayonnaise
- 1 tbsp Dijon mustard
- salt and pepper to taste
- paprika for garnish
- green onion for garnish

Instructions

- Peel the eggs and cut them in half lengthwise.
- Remove the egg yolks and place them in a bowl.
- Mix with mayonnaise, mustard, salt and pepper into a fine mixture.
- Pour the mixture into each egg white and sprinkle with ground paprika and chopped onion.

NUTRITION FACTS (PER SERVING)

Calories	81	
Total Fat	5.2g	7%
Saturated Fat	1.7g	8%
Cholesterol	187mg	62%
Sodium	181mg	8%
Total Carbohydrate	1.9g	1%
Dietary Fiber	0.3g	1%
Total Sugars	1.4g	
Protein	6.4g	

Tips: Beat the cooked egg yolks with chunks of fresh avocado to give them texture and flavor.

Chia Pudding

| Prep time: 5 min | Cook time: 0 min | Servings: 4 |

Ingredients

- 2 cups unsweetened coconut milk
- 2 tbsp honey
- 1 tsp lime juice
- 1 tsp vanilla extract
- 1 pinch of sea salt
- ⅓ cup chia seeds

For serving

- 2 cups cubed tropical fruit by your choice

Instructions

- In a large bowl, whisk together all the pudding ingredients except the chia seeds.
- Stir in the chia seeds, then whisk for 1 minute. Leave to stand for 20 minutes at room temperature and whisk from time to time.
- Cover and refrigerate for at least 3 hours (preferably overnight).
- Stir the pudding vigorously. Add chilled pudding to bowls, garnish with fruit and toasted coconut.

NUTRITION FACTS (PER SERVING)

Calories	325	
Total Fat	29.4g	38%
Saturated Fat	25.5g	127%
Cholesterol	0mg	0%
Sodium	78mg	3%
Total Carbohydrate	17.3g	6%
Dietary Fiber	3.5g	13%
Total Sugars	13g	
Protein	3.2g	

Tips: Chia pudding can be stored for up to 5-7 days in an airtight container in the refrigerator.

Overnight Oats

Prep time: 10 min	Cook time: 0 min	Servings: 2

Ingredients

- 1 cup gluten-free oats (I like Bob's Red Mill)
- 1 cup plain coconut milk
- 1 tbsp flax seeds
- 1 tbsp maple syrup (optional)

Toppings

- 1 tbsp coconut flakes
- 1 tbsp chocolate chips

- *1 tbsp almond butter*
- *berries of your choice*

Instructions

- Combine all the ingredients in a jar with a lid and place them in the refrigerator overnight.
- Cover with your favorite toppings in the morning and enjoy.
- If it is too thick, add a little more coconut milk.

NUTRITION FACTS (PER SERVING)

Calories	398	
Total Fat	10.5g	13%
Saturated Fat	4.6g	23%
Cholesterol	0mg	0%
Sodium	98mg	4%
Total Carbohydrate	65.4g	24%
Dietary Fiber	13.2g	47%
Total Sugars	7g	
Protein	13.8g	

Tips: When making oats overnight, stick to a 2:1 liquid to oatmeal ratio for a pasty consistency.

Carrots Hash Browns

Prep time: 10 min	Cook time: 15 min	Servings: 2

Ingredients

- 1 small carrot
- ½ onion
- salt and pepper, to taste
- 1 tbsp coconut oil

Instructions

- Wash and peel the carrot. Use a grater or food processor to grate the carrot.

- Peel the onion and cut it into small cubes or grate it in a food processor. Stir in the grated carrot and onion. Add salt and pepper to taste.
- Heat the coconut oil in a pan (I prefer cast iron) over medium heat. Take a handful of the mix and place it in the pot.
- Gently press down with a spatula and cook 2-3 minutes or until edges are crisp. Flip and cook for another 2 to 3 minutes.
- Use immediately.

NUTRITION FACTS (PER SERVING)

Calories	80	
Total Fat	6.8g	9%
Saturated Fat	5.9g	29%
Cholesterol	0mg	0%
Sodium	18mg	1%
Total Carbohydrate	5.1g	2%
Dietary Fiber	1.2g	4%
Total Sugars	2.4g	
Protein	0.5g	

Tips: Carrots and onions make a great pair in terms of flavor. You can also add tasty oranges as they will help you get a double dose of vitamin C.

Vegetable Frittata

| Prep time: 10 min | Cook time: 15 min | Servings: 6 |

Ingredients

- 2 tbsp coconut oil
- 1 small green bell pepper, diced
- 1 small red bell pepper, diced
- 1 small zucchini, diced
- ½ red onion, thinly sliced
- 2 cups packed baby kale
- ¼ cup tomatoes, chopped
- 1 clove garlic, sliced
- 10 large eggs, beaten
- kosher salt and freshly ground black pepper

Instructions

- Preheat the oven to 375 ° F.
- Heat oil on a medium nonstick skillet over medium-high heat. Add the bell pepper, zucchini, and onion and cook, stirring occasionally, 6 to 7 minutes, until tender.
- Add the kale, tomatoes and garlic and cook, stirring frequently, for about 1 minute, until the kale is wilted and still bright green.
- Reduce the heat to low and add the eggs, 1 teaspoon of salt and a little ground black pepper. Stir gently to distribute the vegetables. Bake, 13 to 15 minutes, until the eggs are set.
- Let stand 5 minutes, then cut into 6 pieces. Serve with hot sauce.

NUTRITION FACTS (PER SERVING)

Calories	64	
Total Fat	4.6g	6%
Saturated Fat	3.9g	20%
Cholesterol	0mg	0%
Sodium	15mg	1%
Total Carbohydrate	5.5g	2%
Dietary Fiber	1g	4%
Total Sugars	1.6g	
Protein	1.4g	

Tips: You can store a frittata in an airtight container in the refrigerator for up to 1 week.

Eggs with Asparagus

Prep time: 5 min	Cook time: 10 min	Servings: 2

Ingredients

- 1 pound asparagus
- ½-pint cherry tomatoes
- 2 eggs
- 1 tbsp olive oil
- 1 tsp chopped fresh thyme
- salt and pepper to taste

Instructions

- Preheat the oven to 400 ° F. Grease a baking sheet with nonstick cooking spray or use baking paper.

- Distribute the asparagus and cherry tomatoes evenly on the baking sheet. Drizzle the vegetables with olive oil. Season to taste with thyme, salt and pepper.
- Roast in the oven until the asparagus is almost tender and the tomatoes are crumpled, 10 to 12 minutes.
- Crack the eggs over the asparagus. Season each with salt and pepper.
- Return to oven and bake until egg whites are set, but yolks are still moving, another 7 to 8 minutes.
- To serve, arrange asparagus, tomatoes and eggs on two plates.

NUTRITION FACTS (PER SERVING)		
Calories	186	
Total Fat	11.9g	15%
Saturated Fat	2.5g	12%
Cholesterol	164mg	55%
Sodium	71mg	3%
Total Carbohydrate	13g	5%
Dietary Fiber	6g	22%
Total Sugars	7g	
Protein	11.4g	

Tips: Asparagus is a low-calorie vegetable that is an excellent source of essential vitamins and minerals, especially folate and vitamins A, C and K.

Shakshuka

Prep time: 10 min	Cook time: 30 min	Servings: 6

Ingredients

- 1 tbsp olive oil
- 1 medium onion, diced
- 1 red bell pepper, seeded and diced
- 4 garlic cloves, finely chopped
- 2 tsp paprika
- 1 tsp cumin
- ½ tsp chili powder
- 1 28-ounce can whole peeled tomatoes
- 6 large eggs
- salt and pepper, to taste

- *1 small bunch fresh dill, chopped*
- *2small bunch fresh thyme, chopped*

Instructions

- Heat olive oil in a large skillet over medium heat. Add the pepper and chopped onion and cook for 5 minutes or until the onion becomes translucent.
- Add the garlic and spices and cook for another minute.
- Pour the can of tomatoes and the juice into the saucepan and crumble the tomatoes with a large spoon.
- Season with salt and pepper and bring the sauce to a boil.
- Use your large spoon to make small cuts in the sauce and break the eggs into each indentation. Cover the pan and cook, 5 to 8 minutes or until the eggs are cooked to your liking.
- Garnish with chopped dill and thyme.

NUTRITION FACTS (PER SERVING)

Calories 95		
Total Fat 5.2g	7%	
Saturated Fat 1.6g	8%	
Cholesterol 186mg	62%	
Sodium 94mg	4%	
Total Carbohydrate 5.5g		2%
Dietary Fiber 1.2g	4%	
Total Sugars 2.6g		
Protein 7.1g		

Tips: Eggs are a great and inexpensive source of high-quality protein. More than half of an egg's protein is found in egg whites, which also contain vitamin B2 and less fat than the yolk. Eggs are rich in selenium, vitamins D, B6, B12, and minerals like zinc, iron, and copper.

Turkey Stuffed Avocado

Prep time: 10 min	Cook time: 15 min	Servings: 2

Ingredients

- 1 avocado, halved and seeded
- 1 cup chopped cooked turkey
- ¼ cup diced fresh tomato
- 1 tbsp sour cream
- 1 tsp wholegrain mustard
- 1 tsp regular mustard
- 1 tbsp lemon juice
- 1 tbsp chopped fresh basil
- ¼ tsp cayenne pepper
- salt and pepper to taste

Instructions

- Place the turkey, tomato, mustard, sour cream, lemon juice, chopped cilantro and cayenne pepper in a bowl and mix.
- Season to taste with salt and black pepper.
- Pour the mixture into the avocado halves and serve.

NUTRITION FACTS (PER SERVING)

Calories	388	
Total Fat	28.2g	36%
Saturated Fat	6.1g	30%
Cholesterol	57mg	19%
Sodium	162mg	7%
Total Carbohydrate	13.4g	5%
Dietary Fiber	7.1g	25%
Total Sugars	2.2g	
Protein	22.9g	

Tips: Turkey is a very rich source of protein, niacin, vitamin B6 and the amino acid tryptophan. Apart from these nutrients, it also contains zinc and vitamin B12.

Scrambled Eggs

Prep time: 5 min	Cook time: 5 min	Servings: 2

Ingredients

- *4 large eggs*
- *¼ cup coconut milk*
- *salt, to taste*
- *freshly ground white pepper (or black pepper), to taste*
- *1-2 tbsp ghee*

Instructions

- Crack the eggs into a glass bowl and beat them until they turn light yellow.
- Add the milk to the eggs and season with salt and white pepper. Beat the eggs like crazy. If you're not up to it, you can use an electric mixer or a stand mixer with a whisk. Whichever device you use, try to get as much air as possible into the eggs.

- Preheat a solid-bottomed nonstick skillet over medium-low heat. Add the ghee and let it melt.
- When the saucepan is hot enough, pour the eggs into it. Do not stir. Let the eggs cook for up to a minute or until the bottom hardens but does not brown.
- Using a heat-resistant rubber spatula, gently press on the edge of the egg toward the center while tilting the pan to allow the egg, which is still liquid, to sink underneath. Repeat with the other edges until all of the liquid is gone.
- Turn off the heat and keep stirring the egg gently until all the raw parts are firm. Do not break the egg and keep the curd as big as possible. As you add more ingredients, add them quickly.
- Transfer to a plate when the eggs are ready but still moist and soft. Serve immediately and enjoy.

NUTRITION FACTS (PER SERVING)		
Calories	329	
Total Fat	30.7g	39%
Saturated Fat	21.2g	106%
Cholesterol	372mg	124%
Sodium	222mg	10%
Total Carbohydrate	2.5g	1%
Dietary Fiber	0.7g	2%
Total Sugars	1.8g	
Protein	13.3g	

Tips: Make it easy on yourself and cook your eggs in a nonstick sauté pan. Use a heat-resistant silicone spatula, so it doesn't melt or scratch the pan.

Mushroom Omelet

Prep time: 10 min	Cook time: 25 min	Servings: 4

Ingredients

- *6 large eggs*
- *½ cup coconut milk*
- *¼ cup fresh mushrooms, sliced*
- *¼ cup zucchini, sliced*
- *½ onion sliced*
- *1 tbsp fresh basil, minced*
- *sea salt and freshly ground black pepper to taste*

Instructions

- Preheat your oven to 350 F.

- Beat the eggs in a bowl with coconut milk and season with sea salt and black pepper.
- Pour the eggs into a round saucepan or cake pan and distribute the rest of the ingredients on top.
- Place in the oven and bake for 20-25 minutes.

NUTRITION FACTS (PER SERVING)

Calories	102	
Total Fat	7.3g	9%
Saturated Fat	6.3g	32%
Cholesterol	0mg	0%
Sodium	153mg	7%
Total Carbohydrate	3.7g	1%
Dietary Fiber	1.1g	4%
Total Sugars	2.1g	
Protein	6.5g	

Tips: Decide on ingredients for the filling of the omelet; try not to include too many ingredients as this will make the omelet hard to fold.

Granola

Prep time: 10 min	Cook time: 25 min	Servings: 12

Ingredients

- *1 cup raw almonds*
- *1 cup raw cashews*
- *⅓ cup raw pumpkin seeds*
- *⅓ cup raw sunflower seeds*
- *¼ cup unsweetened coconut flakes*
- *¼ cup coconut oil*
- *⅓ cup maple syrup*
- *1 tsp pure vanilla extract*
- *pinch of sea salt*
- *2 tsp ground cinnamon*
- *¾ cup dried cranberries*

Instructions

- Preheat the oven to 275 ° F.
- In a food processor or blender, add the almonds, cashews and coconut flakes to cut them into small pieces. Don't mix too much.
- Heat the coconut oil, honey, cinnamon and salt in a large saucepan over medium heat for about 3 to 5 minutes. Remove from the heat and add the vanilla. Then add the seeds, nuts and coconut flakes and toss to coat.
- Spread the muesli mixture evenly on a baking sheet lined with parchment paper.
- Bake for 20 to 25 minutes or until lightly browned. Remove from the oven and add the dried cranberries. You may need to squeeze them into the grain mixture.
- Let cool for 20 minutes or until everything is set. Separate the granola.

NUTRITION FACTS (PER SERVING)

Calories	216	
Total Fat	16.9g	22%
Saturated Fat	6.7g	33%
Cholesterol	0mg	0%
Sodium	23mg	1%
Total Carbohydrate	13.6g	5%
Dietary Fiber	2.2g	8%
Total Sugars	6.5g	
Protein	4.7g	

Tips: You can store granola in an airtight container or mason jar for up to 2 weeks.

LUNCH

Turkey Fajita Bowl

Prep time: 10 min	Cook time: 10 min	Servings: 4

Ingredients

- 1 ½ tsp oregano
- 1 tbsp chili powder
- ½ tsp garlic, minced
- ½ tsp onion powder
- 1 tsp paprika
- 1 ½ tsp salt
- ¾ tsp black pepper
- 1 ½ tsp cumin
- ½ tsp basil
- 1 ½ pounds turkey cut into bite size pieces
- 1 large onion diced

- *1 red pepper diced*
- *1 yellow or orange pepper diced*
- *2 tbsp coconut oil*

Instructions

- Combine oregano, chili powder, onion powder, garlic, paprika, salt, pepper, cumin and basil in a small bowl. Mix well.
- Put 1 tbsp of coconut oil in a saucepan and add the turkey and half of the spice mix.
- Cook until the turkey is cooked through, stirring frequently, about 7 minutes. Put in a bowl or on a plate.
- Add the remaining coconut oil, onion and peppers to the pan. Spread the rest of the spice mix on top and cook, about 8 to 10 minutes, until tender.
- Serve the turkey, peppers and onions over some lettuce or cauliflower rice and garnish with avocado if desired.

NUTRITION FACTS (PER SERVING)

Calories	332	
Total Fat	9.3g	12%
Saturated Fat	4.5g	22%
Cholesterol	131mg	44%
Sodium	1011mg	44%
Total Carbohydrate	9.8g	4%
Dietary Fiber	2.8g	10%
Total Sugars	4.5g	
Protein	50.9g	

Tips: Here is a prep tip for quick fajita turkey marinade: in a large Ziploc bag, combine all the fajita marinade ingredients and the turkey breasts. Seal tightly and let sit for a few minutes to let the flavors penetrate.

Baked Salmon

Prep time: 5 min	Cook time: 30 min	Servings: 2

Ingredients

- *2 (4 ounce) fillets salmon*
- *1 tsp coconut oil*
- *⅛ tsp Cajun seasoning, or to taste*
- *¼ tsp garlic powder*
- *¼ tsp salt*
- *1 lemon, sliced*
- *½ (16 ounces) package frozen broccoli*

Instructions

- Preheat the oven to 375 degrees F.
- Grease a 9 x 13-inch baking dish.
- Place the salmon fillets at the bottom of the baking dish and sprinkle with coconut oil. Season with Cajun seasoning and garlic powder and salt.
- Garnish with one or two lemon wedges at a time. Place the broccoli around the salmon and season lightly with salt and pepper.
- Cover the plate and bake in a preheated oven for 25 to 30 minutes until the vegetables are tender and the fish flakes easily with a fork.

NUTRITION FACTS (PER SERVING)

Calories	130	
Total Fat	3.5g	4%
Saturated Fat	2.4g	12%
Cholesterol	55mg	18%
Sodium	379mg	16%
Total Carbohydrate	4.5g	2%
Dietary Fiber	1.4g	5%
Total Sugars	1.2g	
Protein	22.1g	

Tips: Salmon is low in fat and is a good source of protein. It is also one of the best sources of vitamin B12, as well as potassium, iron and vitamin D.

Fried Rice

| Prep time: 10 min | Cook time: 10 min | Servings: 4 |

Ingredients

- *1 head cauliflower, cut into florets*
- *2 tbsp coconut oil*
- *1 bunch scallions, thinly sliced*
- *3 garlic cloves, minced*
- *1 tbsp minced fresh ginger*
- *2 carrots, peeled and diced*
- *2 celery stalks, diced*
- *1 red bell pepper, diced*
- *2 tbsp rice vinegar*

- *3 tbsp soy sauce*
- *2 tsp Sriracha, or more to taste*

Garnishes

- *1 tbsp olive oil*
- *4 eggs*
- *salt and freshly ground black pepper*
- *4 tbsp chopped fresh cilantro*
- *4 tbsp thinly sliced scallions*
- *4 tsp sesame seeds*

Instructions

- Preparing the fried rice: In the bowl of a food processor, beat the broccoli for 2 to 3 minutes until the mixture resembles rice. Put aside.
- In a large skillet heat oil over medium heat. Add the scallions, garlic and ginger and sauté for about 1 minute until fragrant.
- Add carrots, celery and red peppers and sauté 9 to 11 minutes, until vegetables are tender.
- Add the broccoli rice to the mixture and sauté for 3 to 5 minutes until it begins to brown.
- Add the rice vinegar, soy sauce and sriracha and stir. Put aside.
- In a medium skillet heat oil over medium to high heat. Crack the eggs directly into the pan and cook until the whites are set, but the yolks are still liquid (3 to 4 minutes). Season each with salt and pepper.
- To serve, divide the broccoli rice among four plates and top each with a fried egg. Garnish each plate with 1 tbsp of cilantro, 1 tbsp of chives and 1 tsp of sesame seeds.

NUTRITION FACTS (PER SERVING)

Calories	150	
Total Fat	7.2g	9%
Saturated Fat	5.9g	30%
Cholesterol	0mg	0%
Sodium	763mg	33%
Total Carbohydrate	17.6g	6%
Dietary Fiber	5.6g	20%
Total Sugars	6.9g	
Protein	5.1g	

Tips: Broccoli is a good source of fiber and protein and contains iron, potassium, calcium, selenium and magnesium, as well as the vitamins A, C, E, K and a good array of B vitamins, including folic acid.

Broccoli Tabbouleh

Prep time: 10 min	Cook time: 0 min	Servings: 4

Ingredients

- *1 med broccoli*
- *1 red pepper, diced*
- *½ cup diced sweet onion*
- *1 bunch parsley, minced*
- *⅓ cup pine nuts, toasted*
- *2 cloves garlic, minced*
- *⅓ cup raisins*
- *⅓ cup fresh lemon juice*
- *¼ cup olive oil*

- ½ cup cucumber, diced
- ½ cup tomato, diced
- salt and pepper to taste
- ½ avocado optional

Instructions

- Chop the broccoli extremely finely to the size of quinoa, for example. Use a food processor for this, but don't over-process it, or it will get mushy. Transfer to a large bowl.
- Pour the rest of your ingredients into the bowl with the cauliflower and mix.
- Serve and enjoy.

NUTRITION FACTS (PER SERVING)

Calories	322	
Total Fat	24.2g	31%
Saturated Fat	3g	15%
Cholesterol	0mg	0%
Sodium	55mg	2%
Total Carbohydrate	26.6g	10%
Dietary Fiber	7.2g	26%
Total Sugars	14.5g	
Protein	6.3g	

Tips: Salt the tomatoes and cucumbers ahead of time, allowing them to sit for 10 minutes before rinsing to remove extra moisture that might otherwise make the salad soggy.

Tofu Lettuce Wraps with Peanut Sauce

Prep time: 10 min	Cook time: 20 min	Servings: 4

Ingredients

- 4-ounce block of tofu
- ½ cup vegetable broth
- ½ tsp soy sauce
- ½ tsp maple syrup
- ⅛ tsp ground coriander
- ⅛ tsp garlic powder
- 4 leaves of butter lettuce
- 1 small carrot, peeled and julienned
- 1 to 1 ½ cups thinly sliced cabbage
- 1 medium red bell pepper, sliced
- peanut sauce

For garnish

- 1 stalk of scallions, sliced (optional)

- *red pepper flakes (optional)*

Instructions

- Cut the tofu into ½-inch cubes and place in a food processor. Blend the tofu for about 5 seconds until you get very small pieces of tofu.
- In a bowl, combine the vegetable broth, soy sauce, maple syrup, garlic powder and ground cilantro.
- Heat a coated skillet or frying pan over medium heat. Add the tofu broth mixture. Cook, stirring occasionally, 8 to 9 minutes, until the liquids are completely absorbed by the tofu.
- It may seem like the tofu is ready to be removed from the stove in 5 minutes, but resist the urge to do so. Once the liquid has been absorbed, remove the saucepan from the heat.
- Assemble the salad buns. Stuff the lettuce leaves with carrots, cabbage, red pepper and tofu. Pour peanut sauce over filling and garnish with sliced chives and paprika flakes, if desired.

NUTRITION FACTS (PER SERVING)

Calories	101	
Total Fat	4.2g	5%
Saturated Fat	0.8g	4%
Cholesterol	0mg	0%
Sodium	216mg	9%
Total Carbohydrate	10.1g	4%
Dietary Fiber	1.5g	5%
Total Sugars	4.7g	
Protein	7.1g	

Tips: The beautiful thing about lettuce wraps is that they are highly customizable in terms of content and wrapping. Cabbage leaves might also make an excellent replacement.

Pumpkin Chili

Prep time: 10 min	Cook time: 250 min	Servings: 4

Ingredients

- *½ lb. grass-fed ground beef*
- *¼ lb. organic ground turkey*
- *¼ tbsp coconut oil*
- *1 small onion diced*
- *1 carrot*
- *1 medium green pepper diced*
- *2 cloves garlic minced*
- *½ tsp sea salt (adjusts to taste)*
- *½ 28 oz. can crushed tomatoes*
- *½ 14.5 oz. can diced tomatoes not drained, no salt added*
- *½ 15 oz. can pumpkin puree*
- *1 tsp ancho chili powder*
- *½ tsp smoked paprika*

- small pinch of chipotle chili powder (adjust to taste)
- ½ tsp cumin
- 1 tsp pumpkin pie spice
- chopped fresh cilantro for garnish if desired

Instructions

- Heat a large skillet over medium heat and add the coconut oil. Add the beef and turkey and break up any lumps so that they are evenly browned. As soon as ⅔ of it looks done, drain the fat (leave a little on it) and add the onion and pepper.
- Stir and continue cooking for 2 min or until the meat is golden brown and the onion and peppers begin to soften. Do not drain more fat. Add the garlic, stir and cook for another minute.
- Reduce the heat and add the grated tomatoes, diced tomatoes, pumpkin, half a teaspoon of salt and seasonings. Stir to combine well, then increase the heat to bring to a boil. After bubbling, bring the heat to a boil, cover and simmer for 45 min to thicken and combine flavors. Garnish with cilantro and avocado, if desired, and serve.

NUTRITION FACTS (PER SERVING)

Calories	251	
Total Fat	9.9g	13%
Saturated Fat	3.7g	18%
Cholesterol	67mg	22%
Sodium	482mg	21%
Total Carbohydrate	19g	7%
Dietary Fiber	6.8g	24%
Total Sugars	10.6g	
Protein	23.4g	

Tips: The taste will improve the longer this chili cooks, which also makes it great for leftovers. You can store leftovers covered in the refrigerator for up to 5 days.

Sautéed Turkey and Cabbage

Prep time: 20 min	Cook time: 20 min	Servings: 4

Ingredients

- 2 turkey breasts, skinless, boneless and sliced
- 1 head of cabbage, shredded
- 2 carrots, shredded
- 3 tbsp paprika
- 3 tomatoes, pureed
- 1 cup chicken stock
- 2 tbsp coconut oil
- sea salt and freshly ground black pepper

Instructions

- Melt the coconut oil in a skillet over medium to high heat.
- Cook the turkey slices until golden brown on each side.
- When you are almost done, add the shredded cabbage and carrots to the pan and cook, stirring, for 4-5 minutes.
- Add the tomatoes, chicken broth, paprika and season to taste.
- Stir everything well and bring to a boil.
- Lower the heat and simmer for 10 to 12 minutes to make sure the turkey is cooked through.
- Remove from the heat and serve hot.

NUTRITION FACTS (PER SERVING)

Calories	172	
Total Fat	8.3g	11%
Saturated Fat	6.2g	31%
Cholesterol	9mg	3%
Sodium	469mg	20%
Total Carbohydrate	20.9g	8%
Dietary Fiber	8.4g	30%
Total Sugars	11.1g	
Protein	7.9g	

Tips: Cabbage is a nutritious vegetable that has many applications and goes well with everything from pork and beef to lamb, chicken, turkey and other poultry.

Spicy Chicken Stew

Prep time: 15 min	Cook time: 8 h	Servings: 4

Ingredients

- 1 tbsp coconut oil
- 1 pound chicken stew meat
- salt and pepper to taste
- 2 cloves garlic, minced
- 1 tsp chopped fresh ginger
- 1 fresh jalapeno pepper, diced
- 1 tbsp curry powder
- 1 (14.5 ounces) can diced tomatoes with juice
- 1 onion, sliced and quartered
- 1 cup chicken broth

Instructions

- Heat the coconut oil in a pan over medium heat and brown the chicken meat on all sides. Remove from the pan, retain the juice and season with salt and pepper.
- Cook the garlic, ginger and jalapeño in the pan for 2 minutes, stir until tender and season with curry powder. Stir in the diced tomatoes with juice.
- Place the onion in the bottom of a slow cooker and cover it with the browned meat. Pour the mixture from the pot into the slow cooker and stir in the chicken broth.
- Cover and cook over low heat for 6 to 8 hours.

NUTRITION FACTS (PER SERVING)

Calories	247	
Total Fat	11.5g	15%
Saturated Fat	4.9g	25%
Cholesterol	71mg	24%
Sodium	380mg	17%
Total Carbohydrate	8.8g	3%
Dietary Fiber	2.6g	9%
Total Sugars	4.2g	
Protein	26.9g	

Tips: The most traditional approach to achieve the characteristic thick texture of stew is to add flour to it. Depending on how thick you prefer, you'll need one to two tablespoons of flour (such as almond or coconut flour) for every cup of liquid.

Stir Fry with Chicken and Cauliflower

Prep time: 10 min	Cook time: 20 min	Servings: 4

Ingredients

- *3 cups cauliflower florets*
- *1 tbsp coconut oil*
- *2 skinless, boneless chicken breast halves - cut into 1-inch strips*
- *¼ cup sliced green onions*
- *4 cloves garlic, thinly sliced*
- *1 tbsp hoisin sauce*
- *1 tbsp chili paste*
- *1 tbsp low sodium soy sauce*
- *½ tsp ground ginger*

- ¼ tsp crushed red pepper
- ½ tsp salt
- ½ tsp black pepper
- ⅛ cup chicken stock

Instructions

- Place the cauliflower in a steamer with over 1 inch of boiling water and cover. Cook 5 minutes until tender but still firm.
- In a skillet, heat the oil over medium heat and brown the chicken, spring onions and garlic until the chicken is no longer pink and the juices run clear.
- Stir in hoisin sauce, chili paste and soy sauce in skillet. Season with ginger, red pepper, salt and black pepper. Add the chicken broth and simmer for about 2 minutes. Add the steamed cauliflower until coated with the sauce mixture.

NUTRITION FACTS (PER SERVING)

Calories	154	
Total Fat	6.3g	8%
Saturated Fat	3.7g	19%
Cholesterol	34mg	11%
Sodium	672mg	29%
Total Carbohydrate	9.5g	3%
Dietary Fiber	2.4g	9%
Total Sugars	4.2g	
Protein	16g	

Tips: Water accounts for 92 grams of the 100 grams of cauliflower in one serving. This indicates that this vegetable can help you stay hydrated and that you can eat a lot of it without sacrificing your body shape. It also has a lot of fiber.

Thai Coconut Broccoli

Prep time: 10 min	Cook time: 10 min	Servings: 4

Ingredients

- 2 heads of broccoli cut into floret chunks
- 1 can coconut milk
- 2 tbsp coconut aminos
- 2 tbsp honey
- 3 tbsp shredded coconut
- sliced serrano chili
- zest of one lime and then cut into chunks for garnish

Instructions

- Place the broccoli, coconut milk, coconut aminos, and honey in a large saucepan. Bring to a boil, then reduce to medium and cook until the coconut milk is reduced by half, about 20 minutes.

- Add the grated coconut and cook for another 10 to 15 minutes or until the broccoli is tender.
- Garnish with sliced serrano chili, lime zest and lime wedges and serve immediately.

NUTRITION FACTS (PER SERVING)		
Calories	212	
Total Fat	15.7g	20%
Saturated Fat	13.8g	69%
Cholesterol	0mg	0%
Sodium	129mg	6%
Total Carbohydrate	19.1g	7%
Dietary Fiber	3.3g	12%
Total Sugars	11.9g	
Protein	2.9g	

Tips: You can easily cook broccoli in water: In a large pot, add water and salt, and then bring water to a boil over high heat. Add the broccoli florets and cook until bright green in color and crisp-tender.

Pumpkin Soup

Prep time: 10 min	Cook time: 15 min	Servings: 6

Ingredients

- 1 tbsp coconut oil
- 1 medium onion, chopped
- 1 large carrot, chopped
- 1 leek, chopped
- 3 cloves of garlic, minced
- 1 medium-sized squash
- 3 cups vegetable broth
- 1 green apple, peeled, cored, and chopped
- ¼ tsp ground cinnamon
- 1 sprig fresh thyme
- 1 sprig fresh rosemary
- 1 tsp kosher salt
- ¼ tsp black pepper
- pinch of nutmeg, optional

Instructions

- Choose to sauté in your Instant Pot. Add coconut oil and sauté onion, carrot, leek and garlic for about 3 to 5 minutes. Add the vegetable broth, pumpkin, apple, cinnamon, thyme, rosemary, salt, pepper and nutmeg if using.
- Place the lid securely on the Instant Pot and turn the knob to close it. Cook under high pressure for 10 minutes and quickly release the pressure.
- Use a hand blender in the instant pot to puree the soup until smooth. If you don't have a hand blender, you can let the soup cool slightly and gently put it in a regular blender and stir until smooth.
- Serve the soup warm, in bowls and garnished with some fresh herbs.

NUTRITION FACTS (PER SERVING)

Calories	142	
Total Fat	3.4g	4%
Saturated Fat	2.3g	11%
Cholesterol	0mg	0%
Sodium	784mg	34%
Total Carbohydrate	26.2g	10%
Dietary Fiber	3.3g	12%
Total Sugars	9.3g	
Protein	5.5g	

Tips: Since an Instant Pot shoots steam straight up, it's always best to use it in an unobstructed or well-circulated place, like under a hood vent. Avoid releasing steam right under cabinets — because repeated exposure to heat and steam can mess with wood and paint.

DINNER

Zucchini Pasta Salad

| Prep time: 15 min | Cook time: 0 min | Servings: 4 |

Ingredients

- 4 medium zucchini spiralized
- 2 cups grape tomatoes sliced in half
- 1 cup red onion diced
- 1 cup brussels sprouts chopped
- 1 green bell pepper diced

For the dressing

- 4 tbsp extra virgin olive oil
- 2 tbsp balsamic vinegar
- 2 tbsp lemon juice

- *2 tbsp minced garlic*
- *3 tbsp basil*

Instructions

- In a bowl, combine the dressing ingredients. Put aside.
- In another large bowl, toss the vegetables for the salad. Drizzle with dressing and serve.
- If not served immediately, keep the dressing separate from the salad until you are ready to eat it.

NUTRITION FACTS (PER SERVING)		
Calories	143	
Total Fat	7.8g	10%
Saturated Fat	1.2g	6%
Cholesterol	0mg	0%
Sodium	35mg	2%
Total Carbohydrate	17.7g	6%
Dietary Fiber	5.5g	20%
Total Sugars	8.5g	
Protein	4.9g	

Tips: Zucchini is packed with many important vitamins, minerals, and antioxidants. It has high fiber content and a low-calorie count.

Roasted Red Pepper Tomato Soup

Prep time: 15 min	Cook time: 30 min	Servings: 4

Ingredients

- 3 red bell peppers quartered
- a drizzle of olive oil
- 1-pound plum tomatoes quartered
- 1 yellow onion quartered
- 4 large garlic cloves
- 1 tbsp coconut oil
- ½ tsp dry parsley
- ½ tsp dry basil
- 3 cups low sodium vegetable broth
- ¼ cup raw almond
- salt and pepper to taste

Instructions

- Preheat oven to 425 F convection baking and line a large baking sheet with parchment paper.
- Arrange your vegetables in a single layer, drizzle with oil and sprinkle with parsley and basil.
- Roast the vegetables for 30 to 40 minutes or until the skin of the pepper is blackened, then take them out of the oven. Once cool to the touch, peel the peppers. The skins peel off easily, but if there are any stubborn lumps, leave them.
- Peel the garlic, it comes out easily after roasting. Put in your blender with all the other ingredients except the sides. Stir everything until smooth, season with salt and pepper and adjust if necessary.
- Serve garnished with fresh basil, croutons, crackers, or black pepper.

NUTRITION FACTS (PER SERVING)

Calories	116	
Total Fat	6.4g	8%
Saturated Fat	3.2g	16%
Cholesterol	0mg	0%
Sodium	329mg	14%
Total Carbohydrate	14.1g	5%
Dietary Fiber	3.3g	12%
Total Sugars	7g	
Protein	2.7g	

Tips: Leftovers can be kept refrigerated for up to 4 days, or you can freeze them in a freezer-safe, air-tight container for up to 3 months.

Eggs and Zoodles

Prep time: 10 min	Cook time: 10 min	Servings: 2

Ingredients

- *nonstick spray*
- *3 zucchinis, spiralizer into noodles*
- *2 tbsp coconut oil*
- *kosher salt and freshly ground black pepper*
- *4 large eggs*
- *paprika, for garnishing*
- *fresh cilantro, for garnishing*

Instructions

- Preheat the oven to 350 ° F. Lightly grease a baking sheet with nonstick spray or use baking paper.
- In a large bowl, combine the zucchini noodles and coconut oil. Season with salt and pepper. Divide into 4 equal portions, place on a baking sheet and nest each.
- Carefully crack an egg in the middle of each nest. Bake for 9 to 11 minutes until the eggs are set. Season with salt and pepper.
- Garnish with ground paprika and chopped cilantro.

NUTRITION FACTS (PER SERVING)		
Calories	310	
Total Fat	24.1g	31%
Saturated Fat	15g	75%
Cholesterol	372mg	124%
Sodium	174mg	8%
Total Carbohydrate	11g	4%
Dietary Fiber	3.5g	13%
Total Sugars	6g	
Protein	16.4g	

Tips: Make your zoodles in advance! This is the best tip to save time. After making several zucchini rolls, line a large plastic or glass container with a paper towel, add the noodles and place them in the refrigerator. They stay fresh for 2-3 days.

Roasted Spiced Cauliflower

Prep time: 5 min	Cook time: 35 min	Servings: 6

Ingredients

- 1 tbsp of coconut oil
- 1 head of cauliflower, trimmed at the base, with green leaves removed
- 1 can almond milk
- juice of 1 lemon
- zest of 1 lemon
- 2 tbsp of chili powder
- 1 tbsp of cumin
- 1 tbsp of garlic minced
- 1 tsp of curry powder
- 2 tsp of sea salt
- 1 tsp of black pepper

Instructions

- Preheat your oven to 400 degrees. Take the coconut oil and place it in a baking dish. Throw it in the oven to melt it.
- Combine the almond milk, lemon zest, lemon juice, chili powder, cumin, garlic powder and curry powder in a bowl. Season with salt and pepper.
- Now take your cauliflower by the head and dip it into the bowl. Brush everything with the marinade. Use your hands to make sure it is well covered all over.
- Place the cauliflower in the baking dish you used to melt the coconut oil. Roast for 30 to 40 minutes until dry and lightly browned. A crust will form on the surface of the cauliflower in the marinade.
- Let it cool for a few minutes before cutting it into pieces and serving!

NUTRITION FACTS (PER SERVING)

Calories	135	
Total Fat	12.2g	16%
Saturated Fat	10.5g	52%
Cholesterol	0mg	0%
Sodium	722mg	31%
Total Carbohydrate	7.1g	3%
Dietary Fiber	2.6g	9%
Total Sugars	2.7g	
Protein	2.3g	

Tips: Cauliflower is a great source of antioxidants and sulforaphane. It also supports our hormonal balance and immune system.

Crispy Sweet Potato Latkes

Prep time: 10 min	Cook time: 15 min	Servings: 22

Ingredients

- *2 pounds sweet potatoes peeled*
- *1 large onion peeled and quartered*
- *2 large eggs*
- *1 ½ tbsp almond flour*
- *1 tsp fine sea salt*
- *½ tsp freshly ground black pepper*
- *½-¾ cup coconut oil, for frying*
- *Scallions or chives thinly sliced, for garnish*

Instructions

- Preheat your oven to 300 ° F and line a large baking sheet with parchment paper. You're not going to cook the latkes, it's just to keep them warm and crisp before serving.

80

- Mash the sweet potatoes and onions with a food processor using a paper shredder or hand grater. If you are using a food processor, you may need to cut the sweet potatoes to fit them properly.
- Line a large bowl with a few layers of paper towels and add the crumbled mixture to the bowl. Squeeze as much water as possible out of the sink. You can do this twice with clean paper towels to remove as much water as possible. After squeezing, remove the paper towels and pour the mixture into a large mixing bowl.
- Add the eggs, almond flour, salt and pepper. Mix with your hands until everything is well combined.
- Heat the oil in a large skillet over medium heat. You will need to set the heat to medium / medium-high as you work to keep the oil at the right temperature. Cover a large plate with paper towels to drain each batch.
- Drop 1-1 / 2-2 round tablespoons of the mixture into the pot and gently crush and squeeze to smooth. It is important not to fill the pan to keep the oil hot.
- Fry until golden brown on one side for about 1-3 minutes (look at them), then gently flip with a spatula. Continue cooking until the second side is golden and crisp, another 1 to 3 minutes. Place on paper towels and drain briefly, then onto the prepared baking sheet. Place in the oven to keep warm while roasting additional batches.
- Repeat with the remaining mixture until used; Depending on the size, you get between 22 and 26. Serve immediately with chives or spring onions, applesauce or ranch (or keep warm in the oven).

NUTRITION FACTS (PER SERVING)

Calories	61	
Total Fat	5.2g	7%
Saturated Fat	4.1g	20%
Cholesterol	16mg	5%
Sodium	88mg	4%
Total Carbohydrate	3.5g	1%
Dietary Fiber	0.5g	2%
Total Sugars	0.9g	
Protein	0.9 g	

Tips: Sweet potatoes are a great source of fiber, vitamins, and minerals.

Cabbage Chips

Prep time: 10 min	Cook time: 2 hours	Servings: 6

Ingredients

- *1 head of cabbage, red or green (savoy works well)*
- *coconut oil*
- *sea salt*

Instructions

- Preheat the oven to 200 ° F / 93 ° C.
- Cut the cabbage in half and cut the core. Separate the cabbage leaves. Cut large leaves into halves or quarters.
- Place cabbage leaves on wire racks on baking sheets.
- Bake until crisp. Smaller (thinner) sheets will take about 2 hours, larger (thicker) sheets may take up to 3 hours.
- When the leaves are cooked, brush with coconut oil and sprinkle with sea salt and dill.

NUTRITION FACTS (PER SERVING)

Calories	72	
Total Fat	2.5g	3%
Saturated Fat	2g	10%
Cholesterol	0mg	0%
Sodium	115mg	5%
Total Carbohydrate	12.1g	4%
Dietary Fiber	5.2g	19%
Total Sugars	6.7g	
Protein	2.7g	

Tips: Many studies have suggested that increasing the consumption of plant-based foods like cabbage decreases the risk of diabetes, obesity, heart disease, and overall mortality. It can also help promote a healthy complexion, increased energy, and overall lower weight.

Healthy Carrot Fries

| Prep time: 5 min | Cook time: 35 min | Servings: 4 |

Ingredients

- *8 large carrots*
- *1 tbsp coconut oil*
- *1 tsp garlic powder*
- *salt and pepper, to taste*
- *optional topping: fresh cilantro*

Almond Dipping Sauce

- *½ cup raw almond, soaked*
- *1 ½ tbsp red curry paste*
- *1 tbsp coconut aminos*
- *2 tbsp lime juice*
- *½ tsp garlic powder*

- ½ *tsp red pepper flakes*
- ½ *tsp ginger*
- ¼ *cup water*

Instructions

- Soak the almonds the night before. Put them in a small bowl and cover with water. If you forgot to soak them, add them to hot water while the carrots are cooking.
- Preheat the oven to 375 degrees F. Cut the carrots into matchsticks. Transfer to a large bowl and toss with coconut oil, garlic powder, salt and pepper. Place on two baking sheets lined with parchment paper and distribute evenly. Make sure they aren't too close together.
- Bake for 20 minutes, stir / flip and bake another 15 minutes.
- While the fried carrots are cooking, prepare the sauce. Put all the ingredients in a blender and stir until smooth.
- As soon as the carrots are ready, sprinkle with fresh cilantro.

NUTRITION FACTS (PER SERVING)

Calories	171	
Total Fat	9.4g	12%
Saturated Fat	3.4g	17%
Cholesterol	0mg	0%
Sodium	106mg	5%
Total Carbohydrate	20.4g	7%
Dietary Fiber	5.3g	19%
Total Sugars	8.1g	
Protein	3.9g	

Tips: Carrots are a good source of antioxidants, fiber and vitamin K1.

Sautéed Spinach with Stuffed Mushrooms

| Prep time: 5 min | Cook time: 35 min | Servings: 6 |

Ingredients

- *6 mushrooms*
- *2 spring onions*
- *1 lb. ground chicken*
- *⅛ tsp turmeric*
- *½ tsp garlic powder*
- *handful of spinach*
- *sea salt*
- *1-2 tbsp avocado oil*

Instructions

- First, remove the stems from the mushrooms and cut them finely.
- Then chop the spring onions.

- Fry over medium heat and add ½ tbsp avocado oil. Brown the mushrooms, garlic powder and spring onions. Add the turmeric. Once the onions are tender, about a minute or two, add the ground chicken. Cook the meat well. Add the spinach last until it wilts.
- Fill the mushroom caps with the ground chicken mixture and bake at 250F for 5 minutes.
- Serve and enjoy.

NUTRITION FACTS (PER SERVING)

Calories	65	
Total Fat	2.5g	3%
Saturated Fat	0.7g	3%
Cholesterol	25mg	8%
Sodium	125mg	5%
Total Carbohydrate	1.7g	1%
Dietary Fiber	0.6g	2%
Total Sugars	0.6g	
Protein	9g	

Tips: Mushrooms are a rich, low-calorie source of fiber, protein, and antioxidants. They may also mitigate the risk of developing serious health conditions, such as Alzheimer's, heart disease, cancer, and diabetes.

Blueberry Muffins

Prep time: 10 min	Cook time: 15 min	Servings: 12

Ingredients

- 1 cup almond butter
- 1 cup applesauce
- 2 tbsp coconut oil, melted
- ¼ cup honey
- 2 large eggs
- ½ tsp baking powder
- 1 tsp pure vanilla extract
- ½ cup blueberries

Instructions

- Preheat oven to 400 ° F. Grease 12 muffin cups with nonstick spray or baking paper.
- In the bowl of a blender, puree the almond butter, applesauce, coconut oil, honey, eggs, baking powder and vanilla extract.
- Spread the batter on the prepared muffin bowls. Distribute the blueberries and chocolate pieces evenly over the muffins.
- Bake for 12 to 15 minutes until a toothpick inserted into the muffin comes out clean.
- Let cool for at least 5 minutes before serving.

NUTRITION FACTS (PER SERVING)		
Calories	83	
Total Fat	3.9g	5%
Saturated Fat	2.3g	11%
Cholesterol	31mg	10%
Sodium	12mg	1%
Total Carbohydrate	11.6g	4%
Dietary Fiber	0.8g	3%
Total Sugars	9g	
Protein	1.6g	

Tips: As a general rule, fill your muffin cups about ¾ full. That should leave enough room for the muffins to rise without making a mess.

Porridge

Prep time: 5 min	Cook time: 15 min	Servings: 2

Ingredients

- *2–3 tbsp lightly toasted sunflower seeds*
- *2 tbsp unsweetened shredded coconut*
- *1 tbsp flaxseed*
- *½ tsp cinnamon*
- *1 tsp ginger, ground*
- *pinch of turmeric, ground*
- *pinch of sea salt*
- *½ cup coconut milk, more if needed*
- *1 cup chopped butter squash, cooked*

Instructions

- Combine all the dry ingredients (sunflower seeds, coconut chia and spices) and grind in a coffee grinder or blender to get a floury consistency. If you are short on time, use tahini instead of sunflower seeds and mix the ingredients).
- Set aside a part of the dry mixture for garnish.
- In a small bowl, combine the dry mixture with water or coconut milk, let it adsorb and form a gel. Don't hesitate to keep some gel to cover the dish at the end!
- Put the cooked butternut squash mixture in a blender and stir until smooth.
- Heat the porridge on the stove over medium heat until it begins to bubble. Stir occasionally.
- Remove from the heat, pour into your favorite bowl and top with the dry mixture you set aside.
- Garnish with fresh berries or honey, depending on your taste.

NUTRITION FACTS (PER SERVING)		
Calories	384	
Total Fat	31.3g	40%
Saturated Fat	17.4g	87%
Cholesterol	0mg	0%
Sodium	144mg	6%
Total Carbohydrate	21.8g	8%
Dietary Fiber	6.5g	23%
Total Sugars	12.5g	
Protein	8.2g	

Tips: Porridge is a gluten-free whole grain and a great source of important vitamins, minerals, fiber and antioxidants.

Matcha Chia Pudding with Berries

Prep time: 5 min	Cook time: 0 min	Servings: 2

Ingredients

- 2 tsp matcha green tea powder
- 1 cup almond milk
- ¼ cup chia seeds
- ½ tbsp honey
- raspberries and almonds for garnish

Instructions

- In a large bowl, combine the matcha green tea powder with the almond milk and beat until smooth.

- Add the chia seeds and honey. Stir to combine, making sure there are no clumps of chia seeds. Put it in the fridge for 2 hours or overnight.
- Garnish with raspberries and almonds or other fruit and nuts to taste.

NUTRITION FACTS (PER SERVING)

Calories	312	
Total Fat	29.7g	38%
Saturated Fat	25.5g	127%
Cholesterol	0mg	0%
Sodium	19mg	1%
Total Carbohydrate	12.5g	5%
Dietary Fiber	4.9g	17%
Total Sugars	8.3g	
Protein	4.4g	

Tips: You can freeze the chia seed pudding for up to 3 months in individual servings. Use freezer-safe zip lock bags or small mason jar containers. To thaw, just place it in the fridge overnight.

DESSERT

Beet Brownies

Prep time: 20 min	Cook time: 35 min	Servings: 8 pieces

Ingredients

- ¼ cup coconut oil, plus more for pan
- 3 oz. bittersweet chocolate, chopped
- ¼ cup honey
- 4 oz. cooked peeled whole beets, pureed in blender or food processor
- ½ tsp pure vanilla extract
- ½ tsp espresso powder
- ⅛ tsp Kosher salt
- 1 large egg, at room temperature
- ¼ cup almond flour

Instructions

- Preheat the oven to 350 ° F.

- Butter an 8-inch square baking dish and line the bottom with parchment paper, leaving protrusions on each side.
- Melt chocolate and half a cup of butter in a medium saucepan over low heat, stirring occasionally, until smooth.
- Remove from the heat, let cool slightly, then add the honey, beets, vanilla, espresso powder and salt. Beat the eggs one at a time until they are completely incorporated.
- Stir in the almond flour until everything is combined.
- Pour the batter into the prepared baking dish and bake for 30 to 35 minutes, until the knife inserted in the center comes out clean or with just a few damp crumbs.
- Let cool in the pan for 10 minutes then transfer to the cutting board with the overhangs. Cut into 8 squares.

NUTRITION FACTS (PER SERVING)

Calories	174	
Total Fat	11.6g	15%
Saturated Fat	8.2g	41%
Cholesterol	2mg	1%
Sodium	71mg	3%
Total Carbohydrate	16.6g	6%
Dietary Fiber	0.9g	3%
Total Sugars	14.8g	
Protein	1.6g	

Tips: Beets are rich in iron, an essential part of red blood cells. Without iron, red blood cells cannot carry oxygen around the body.

Pumpkin Brownies

Prep time: 15 min	Cook time: 40 min	Servings: 16

Ingredients

- 2 cups pumpkin, peeled and diced
- ¼ cup honey
- ½ cup cocoa powder
- 2 tbsp smooth grass-fed cow butter (or coconut butter)
- ¾ cup unsweetened soy milk
- pinch of salt to taste
- 2 cups ground walnuts
- 2 tsp baking powder

Instructions

- Preheat the oven to 360 F.

- Put the pumpkin in a saucepan and cover with water. Bring to a boil and simmer for 15 minutes, until tender enough to be lightly pricked with a fork. Drain the pumpkin.
- Place the cooked pumpkin, honey, cocoa powder, peanut butter, coconut milk and salt in a food processor or blender.
- Gently mix everything until well combined.
- And coconut flour and baking powder and mix briefly just to combine.
- Transfer the mixture to a square or rectangular baking dish lined with greased parchment paper. I used a 23cm square mold.
- Bake for 25 minutes. They should be slightly cracked on the top and slightly firm on the inside but still quite sticky. Be careful not to cook for too long. Let cool before dicing.

NUTRITION FACTS (PER SERVING)

Calories	101	
Total Fat	4.3g	6%
Saturated Fat	3.1g	15%
Cholesterol	0mg	0%
Sodium	29mg	1%
Total Carbohydrate	16.5g	6%
Dietary Fiber	3.6g	13%
Total Sugars	6.1g	
Protein	2g	

Tips: Make sure you don't underbake or overbake your brownies because that makes all the difference. Always follow your recipe's baking time (toothpick test doesn't work here!) and bake your brownies until they're done. Leftover brownies can stay in the refrigerator for up to 2 or 3 days.

Mint Chocolate Chip Cupcakes

Prep time: 5 min	Cook time: 15 min	Servings: 9

Ingredients

- 6 tbsp organic cocoa
- ¼ cup flax seed flour
- ½ cup almond flour
- 1 tsp baking powder
- ¼ tsp baking soda
- 2 eggs
- 1 tsp peppermint extract or 2–3 drops of peppermint essential oil
- ½ cup almond milk
- ½ cup honey

Avocado mint frosting

- 1 large avocado

- *⅓ cup coconut butter*
- *½ drops of peppermint essential oil or ½ –1 tsp peppermint extract*

Instructions

- Preheat the oven to 360 F.
- Combine the dry ingredients in a bowl. Add wet ingredients, one by one and stir until the dough is smooth.
- Place the cupcakes in the cupcake molds.
- Bake for 15 to 16 minutes. Or until a toothpick inserted in the middle comes out clean.
- Carefully remove the cupcakes from the pan to cool them on the wire rack.

Avocado frosting

- Mix everything in a blender. Adjust the sweetness and mint to taste.
- Pour the icing over the cupcakes. Garnish with chocolate chips.

NUTRITION FACTS (PER SERVING)

Calories	235	
Total Fat	14.9g	19%
Saturated Fat	5.1g	25%
Cholesterol	41mg	14%
Sodium	61mg	3%
Total Carbohydrate	25.9g	9%
Dietary Fiber	5g	18%
Total Sugars	18.5g	
Protein	5.2g	

Tips: To replace almond flour, I recommend using chestnut flour or any other gluten-free flour blend.

Apple Cinnamon Granola Bars

Prep time: 20 min	Cook time: 0 min	Servings: 20

Ingredients

- *1 cup raw walnuts*
- *1 cup raw almonds*
- *1 cup raw cashews*
- *1 cup coconut flakes, unsweetened*
- *1 tbsp cinnamon*
- *¼ tsp nutmeg*
- *⅛ tsp allspice optional*
- *½ tsp sea salt*
- *1 cup dried apples chopped*

- ¼ *cup coconut oil*
- ¼ *cup smooth almond butter*
- ¼ *cup honey*
- *1 tsp pure vanilla extract*

Instructions

- Put all the nuts in a food processor and pulse several times to crush them into a crumbly texture. A few larger pieces are good - don't mix them up too much!
- Transfer the nuts to a large mixing bowl and add the coconut flakes, cinnamon, salt and dried apples to mix evenly.
- Put the melted coconut oil in another bowl and mix in the almond butter, honey and vanilla.
- Pour the wet mixture into a large bowl with the dry ingredients and stir to combine well. Mix well to make sure all of the dry ingredients are covered.
- Line an 8 x 8 or 9 x 9 square pan with baking paper along the bottom and sides, with an extra side facing up for easy removal. Transfer the mixture and press firmly into the pan with your hands or another piece of parchment paper.
- Cover the top with parchment paper or plastic wrap and place in the freezer for at least 30 minutes to set it up, preferably longer if you have time.
- Cut into 20 bars with a long, very sharp knife.
- The bars start to melt at room temperature due to the coconut oil, so they should be kept cold to stay firm.

NUTRITION FACTS (PER SERVING)

Calories	186	
Total Fat	15.3g	20%
Saturated Fat	6.2g	31%
Cholesterol	0mg	0%
Sodium	59mg	3%
Total Carbohydrate	10.4g	4%
Dietary Fiber	2.5g	9%
Total Sugars	5.6g	
Protein	4g	

Tips: When you "press" the mixture into the pan, you really want to pack it in tightly, or your bars will turn out crumbly. Once done, you can wrap the bars in parchment paper and store them one at a time in the refrigerator for up to two weeks.

Banana Bread

Prep time: 10 min	Cook time: 50 min	Servings: 10

Ingredients

- 3 cups applesauce
- 3 large eggs room temp
- ¼ cup maple syrup
- ¼ cup almond milk room temp, blend first if separated
- 1 tsp pure vanilla extract
- ½ cup almond flour sifted
- 2 tbsp tapioca flour
- 6 tbsp raw cacao powder sifted
- 1 tsp baking soda

- ¼ *tsp sea salt*
- ½ *cup dark (vegan) chocolate chips*

Instructions

- Preheat your oven to 350 F and line a medium loaf pan with parchment paper (I used this 8.5 by 4.5 loaf pan).
- Gently combine all the dry ingredients (except the chocolate chips) in the mixing bowl. Be sure to sift the almond flour and cocoa powder before mixing, as they can form lumps.
- In a larger mixing bowl, combine the applesauce with the eggs, almond milk, maple syrup and vanilla. Wet ingredients should be as close to room temperature as possible before starting.
- Gently mix the dry and wet ingredients with a spatula or wooden spoon.
- The batter should not be mixed or stirred vigorously, as this will interfere with the rising of the bread. The batter should be relatively thick and lumpy after mixing.
- Add about ⅓ cup of the chocolate chips, transfer the batter to a prepared loaf pan and distribute it evenly. Spread the remaining chocolate chips on top.
- Bake in preheated oven for 50 to 60 min or until a toothpick comes out in the middle of the bread without dough (melted chocolate is fine).
- Let the bread cool in the pan for 15 min, then gently transfer it to a saucepan holding two sides of the parchment paper to help you.
- Allow bread to cool completely to room temperature before slicing.

NUTRITION FACTS (PER SERVING)

Calories	152	
Total Fat	5.3g	7%
Saturated Fat	1.7g	8%
Cholesterol	0mg	0%
Sodium	189mg	8%
Total Carbohydrate	23.9g	9%
Dietary Fiber	3.7g	13%
Total Sugars	12.4g	
Protein	4.1g	

Tips: Do not open the oven during baking unless you have to – otherwise, the bread might not rise correctly. Leftovers can be stored covered in the refrigerator for up to 2 or 3 days.

Nut Cups

Prep time: 15 min	Cook time: 10 min	Servings: 24

Ingredients

- *1 cup dairy-free chocolate chips*
- *2 tbsp coconut oil*
- *¾ cup chocolate almond butter*

Instructions

- Place the chocolate chips and coconut oil in a microwave-safe bowl. Melt for 45 seconds at 50 % power. Stir very well and continue to melt at 50 % power 20 seconds apart until completely melted. Stir with each heating.
- When the chocolate melts, use a spoon to pour the chocolate into 24 mini paper cupcakes. After adding the chocolate, take each coating and roll the chocolate around the bottom and sides of the paper coating. Then place them on a baking sheet.

- When all 24 are cooked, put them in the freezer for 15 minutes to harden the chocolate.
- When the chocolate is ready, fill the cups with the chocolate almond butter distributed evenly over the 24 cups. Use a spoon or your finger to smooth the butter, then cover each cup with the remaining chocolate. Put in the freezer for 15 minutes to set the chocolate.
- Serve cold or bring to room temperature for a few minutes.

NUTRITION FACTS (PER SERVING)		
Calories	85	
Total Fat	5.4g	7%
Saturated Fat	3.6g	18%
Cholesterol	0mg	0%
Sodium	21mg	1%
Total Carbohydrate	8.5g	3%
Dietary Fiber	1.4g	5%
Total Sugars	6.1g	
Protein	0.9g	

Tips: Before removing the cups from the freezer, make sure the chocolate is fully frozen. If not, they will begin to break down.

Dried Fruit Bars

Prep time: 15 min	Cook time: 10 min	Servings: 4

Ingredients

- 1 cup dried Medjool date, pitted
- ½ cup raw almonds
- ½ cup cashew
- ½ cup dried cranberries
- ½ cup dried blueberries

Instructions

- Preheat your oven to 400 F.

- Place the almonds, cashew in a baking dish and bake for 8-10 minutes. Let cool before use.
- In a food processor, combine all the ingredients and squeeze until the ingredients form a ball. Scrape the edges of the bowl to prevent the mixture from sticking.
- Line a baking sheet with parchment paper. Distribute the mixture in the saucepan and form a large rectangle.
- Cover with another piece of parchment paper and refrigerate for at least 1 hour.
- Cut evenly into bars.

NUTRITION FACTS (PER SERVING)

Calories	166	
Total Fat	10g	13%
Saturated Fat	1.2g	6%
Cholesterol	0mg	0%
Sodium	2mg	0%
Total Carbohydrate	19.5g	7%
Dietary Fiber	3.4g	12%
Total Sugars	10.5g	
Protein	4.2g	

Tips: Store in the refrigerator in an air-tight container and refrigerate for up to 2 weeks.

Cocoa Balls

| Prep time: 5 min | Cook time: 5 min | Servings: 16 |

Ingredients

- 1 cup coconut butter
- ¼ cup vegan cocoa powder
- ⅓ cup honey
- ½ tsp vanilla extract
- ⅛ tsp salt
- 3 to 5 tsp almond flour
- ½ cup mini vegan chocolate chips

Instructions

- Mix everything except the almond flour and chocolate chips.

- Add 3 tbsp of almond flour. Stir for about a minute or until firm and you can roll the mixture into balls. If it still doesn't seem firm enough to form into balls, let the mixture sit for about 5 minutes to give the almond flour time to absorb the moisture. Then add more almond flour if needed.
- Add the chocolate chips. Roll into sixteen 23-gram (about 1") balls.
- Eat immediately or store in an airtight container for up to 1 week, refrigerate for 2 weeks or freeze for 3 months.

NUTRITION FACTS (PER SERVING)

Calories	125	
Total Fat	8.5g	11%
Saturated Fat	1.2g	6%
Cholesterol	0mg	0%
Sodium	23mg	1%
Total Carbohydrate	10.6g	4%
Dietary Fiber	2g	7%
Total Sugars	6.6g	
Protein	4.4g	

Tips: Add an almond in the center. It will taste just like an Almond Joy Candy Bar!

Raspberry Muffin Energy Balls

Prep time: 15 min	Cook time: 00 min	Servings: 10 pieces

Ingredients

- 1 cup almonds
- ½ cup prunes,
- ½ cup dried raspberries
- ½ tsp almond extract
- Zest of 1 lemon
- ¼ tsp sea salt

Instructions

- Place the almonds in the food processor. Process until the almonds are the size of a pea.

- Add prunes and dried raspberries and toss for about 1 to 2 minutes until all the ingredients are broken down and slightly sticky.
- Add the almond extract, lemon zest and salt. Mix until all ingredients have crumbled into a sticky ball.
- You may need to scrape the pages every minute. The process should take 3-5 minutes.
- Roll into balls and store in the refrigerator for up to 2 weeks or in the freezer for several months.

NUTRITION FACTS (PER SERVING)		
Calories	84	
Total Fat	4.9g	6%
Saturated Fat	0.4g	2%
Cholesterol	0mg	0%
Sodium	48mg	2%
Total Carbohydrate	9.2g	3%
Dietary Fiber	2.6g	9%
Total Sugars	5.5g	
Protein	2.4g	

Tips: Almonds are known for reducing bad cholesterol levels, moisturizing and protecting your skin, providing you with iron, protecting you against heart diseases, and reducing your chance of diabetes.

Honey Roasted Walnuts

Prep time: 5 min	Cook time: 10 min	Servings: 4

Ingredients

- 2 cups raw walnuts
- 1½ tbsp honey
- ½ tsp ground nutmeg
- ¼ tsp sea salt

Instructions

- Preheat the oven to 400 ° F. Then line a baking sheet with parchment paper and set aside.

- Place the walnuts, honey, and nutmeg in a large bowl and toss to make sure everything is completely covered.
- Then distribute the nuts on a baking sheet and sprinkle abundantly with sea salt.
- Grill at 400 ° F for 10 minutes.
- Let cool for at least 10 minutes before removing it from the pot and storing it in a Tupperware glass or jar.

NUTRITION FACTS (PER SERVING)

Calories	412	
Total Fat	37g	47%
Saturated Fat	2.2g	11%
Cholesterol	0mg	0%
Sodium	119mg	5%
Total Carbohydrate	12.8g	5%
Dietary Fiber	4.3g	15%
Total Sugars	7.2g	
Protein	15.1g	

Tips: According to a study, eating nuts may help raise your iron levels, lower your bad cholesterol and triglyceride levels, increase the quality of your artery lining, and battle inflammation, which is connected to heart disease.

Sweet Carrot Cake

| Prep time: 30 min | Cook time: 50 min | Servings: 3 |

Ingredients

- *3 eggs*
- *3 tbsp honey*
- *1 carrot*
- *zest of ½ orange*
- *juice of ¼ orange*
- *1 ½ cups coconut flour*

Instructions

- Preheat the oven to 325 F. Separate egg whites and yolks.

- Put the carrot in a pot of boiling water and cook until the carrots are tender. Drain it and mash it with a food processor of forks.
- Mix the carrot puree with the orange zest, orange juice and coconut flour.
- In another bowl, beat the egg yolks and honey and mix with the carrot and flour mixture.
- In another bowl, beat the egg whites into the snow. Using a spatula, gently fold the snow into the flour mixture.
- Grease a 9-inch round cake pan and pour batter into it.
- Bake for about 50 minutes.
- Let cool for 15 minutes before opening the feather pan so that the cake does not stick.
- Cut into pieces and serve hot.

NUTRITION FACTS (PER SERVING)

Calories	198	
Total Fat	6.5g	8%
Saturated Fat	2.9g	14%
Cholesterol	196mg	65%
Sodium	114mg	5%
Total Carbohydrate	27.2g	10%
Dietary Fiber	4.3g	16%
Total Sugars	19.2g	
Protein	8.3g	

Tips: Use real food to naturally color your frosting for cake and cookies. You know when the cake is cooked, when the toothpick inserted in the middle of it comes out clean.

DRINKS

Green Keto Smoothie

Prep time: 5 min	Cook time: 0 min	Servings: 1

Ingredients

- ½ oz. kale leaves
- ¼ avocado (peeled and stone removed)
- 1 small stick celery (chopped)
- 1 cucumber (peeled)
- 1 cup unsweetened coconut milk
- 1 tbs. almond butter
- 1 tbsp freshly squeezed lemon juice

Instructions

- Place all ingredients in a blender.
- Blend until smooth.

- Serve and enjoy!

NUTRITION FACTS (PER SERVING)

Calories	314	
Total Fat	23.3g	30%
Saturated Fat	6.9g	34%
Cholesterol	0mg	0%
Sodium	30mg	1%
Total Carbohydrate	26.4g	10%
Dietary Fiber	8.1g	29%
Total Sugars	11.9g	
Protein	7.1g	

Tips: Kale contains more calcium, vitamin K, and vitamin C than spinach. Spinach, on the other hand, contains more iron, magnesium, potassium, zinc, folate, and vitamins A and E. Overall, both are incredibly nutritious options.

Pomegranate Smoothie

| Prep time: 5 min | Cook time: 0 min | Servings: 1 |

Ingredients

- *1 cup pomegranate juice*
- *½ cup almond milk*
- *1 cup frozen blueberries*

Instructions

- Place all ingredients in a blender.
- Blend until smooth.
- Serve and enjoy!

NUTRITION FACTS (PER SERVING)

Calories	288	
Total Fat	2.6g	3%
Saturated Fat	0.3g	1%
Cholesterol	0mg	0%
Sodium	95mg	4%
Total Carbohydrate	69.1g	25%
Dietary Fiber	8.1g	29%
Total Sugars	45.8g	
Protein	4.7g	

Tips: Add some Chia seeds to the mix as they are a rich source of protein, omega-3s, and antioxidants.

Mint And Citrus Drink

Prep time: 10 min	Cook time: 0 min	Servings: 4

Ingredients

- 1 lemon, sliced
- 2 limes, sliced
- ¼ cup fresh lemon juice
- ¼ cup fresh mint leaves
- 2 liters water
- 1 cup ice

Instructions

- For the lemon juice at the bottom of a jug.

- Add the lemon wedges, limes and mint leaves.
- Pour in the water and stir everything well.
- Add ice and serve immediately, or store ice and refrigerate until ready to serve.

NUTRITION FACTS (PER SERVING)

Calories	20	
Total Fat	0.3g	0%
Saturated Fat	0.2g	1%
Cholesterol	0mg	0%
Sodium	21mg	1%
Total Carbohydrate	5.7g	2%
Dietary Fiber	1.8g	6%
Total Sugars	1.3g	
Protein	0.7g	

Tips: This drink is great for cleansing your body. One of the major benefits of drinking lemon water is that it aids in weight loss and gives your body natural electrolytes.

Super Food Smoothie

Prep time: 5 min	Cook time: 0 min	Servings: 1

Ingredients

- *½ cup frozen berries*
- *1 tbsp hemp seed*
- *1 tbsp coconut oil*
- *1 big handful spinach*
- *1 cup unsweetened almond milk*

Instructions

- Place all ingredients in a blender.
- Blend until smooth.
- Serve and enjoy!

NUTRITION FACTS (PER SERVING)		
Calories	393	
Total Fat	24.7g	32%
Saturated Fat	12.6g	63%
Cholesterol	0mg	0%
Sodium	205mg	9%
Total Carbohydrate	39.5g	14%
Dietary Fiber	7.7g	28%
Total Sugars	19.6g	
Protein	8.7g	

Tips: Banana is the magical smoothie fruit. It has a subtle flavor, so it won't overpower the other flavors and it makes the smoothie dense. You can add it to the smoothie. Just make sure it is not too ripe.

Minty Morning Green Smoothie

| Prep time: 10 min | Cook time: 0 min | Servings: 2 |

Ingredients

- ½ frozen banana
- ½ small avocado
- 1 cup of baby spinach
- ½ raw cucumber
- ½ cup coconut milk
- ½ cup water
- 1 tbsp fresh mint
- ½ squeezed lemon juice
- 1 tbsp maple syrup

Instructions

- Place all ingredients in a high-speed blender.
- Blend until smooth.
- Serve and enjoy!

NUTRITION FACTS (PER SERVING)

Calories	414	
Total Fat	29.2g	37%
Saturated Fat	25.5g	128%
Cholesterol	0mg	0%
Sodium	52mg	2%
Total Carbohydrate	41.1g	15%
Dietary Fiber	6g	21%
Total Sugars	26.5g	
Protein	5.5g	

Tips: Cucumbers contain magnesium, potassium, and vitamin K. These 3 nutrients are vital for the proper functioning of the cardiovascular system.

Coconut Strawberry Drink

Prep time: 10 min	Cook time: 0 min	Servings: 2

Ingredients

- *8 oz. coconut water*
- *¼ cup fresh lime or lemon juice*
- *12 oz. frozen strawberries*
- *8 oz. crushed ice*

Instructions

- Place all ingredients in a high-speed blender.

- Blend until smooth.
- Serve and enjoy!

NUTRITION FACTS (PER SERVING)

Calories	85	
Total Fat	0.5g	1%
Saturated Fat	0.4g	2%
Cholesterol	0mg	0%
Sodium	125mg	5%
Total Carbohydrate	19.5g	7%
Dietary Fiber	4.8g	17%
Total Sugars	13.6g	
Protein	1.1g	

Tips: With only 45 calories in a cup, coconut water is a great substitute for higher-calorie drinks like sodas or juice.

Turmeric Smoothie

Prep time: 5 min	Cook time: 0 min	Servings: 1

Ingredients

- 2 oranges, peeled and coarsely chopped
- 1 small zucchini
- ½ inch fresh ginger, peeled
- ½ tsp ground turmeric
- 1 cup cold water
- 1 tsp maple syrup (optional)

Instructions

- Place all ingredients in a blender.
- Blend until smooth.
- Serve immediately and enjoy!

NUTRITION FACTS (PER SERVING)

Calories	216	
Total Fat	0.8g	1%
Saturated Fat	0.2g	1%
Cholesterol	0mg	0%
Sodium	20mg	1%
Total Carbohydrate	53g	19%
Dietary Fiber	10.5g	37%
Total Sugars	40.5g	
Protein	5.1g	

Tips: If you will use fresh turmeric root – peel it and either cut it into small pieces or grate it.

Parsley Green Smoothie

Prep time: 5 min	Cook time: 0 min	Servings: 1

Ingredients

- *1 small bunch fresh parsley*
- *½ medium avocado*
- *1 green apple*
- *½ tsp honey*
- *1 cup coconut water*

Instructions

- Place all ingredients in a blender.

- Blend until smooth.
- Serve and enjoy!

NUTRITION FACTS (PER SERVING)

Calories	475	
Total Fat	21g	27%
Saturated Fat	4.7g	23%
Cholesterol	0mg	0%
Sodium	267mg	12%
Total Carbohydrate	75.9g	28%
Dietary Fiber	18.2g	65%
Total Sugars	44.5g	
Protein	5.8g	

Tips: Eating apples can support your immune system as apples include various vitamins, such as C and K, minerals and fiber. Studies indicate that eating apples can play a role in preventing cancer, reducing harmful levels of cholesterol and reducing blood pressure.

Chia Smoothie

| Prep time: 10 min | Cook time: 0 min | Servings: 4 |

Ingredients

- *1 tbsp chia seeds*
- *¾ cups unsweetened coconut milk, divided*
- *¾ cups frozen blueberries*

Instructions

- Place all ingredients in a blender.
- Blend until smooth.

- Serve and enjoy!

NUTRITION FACTS (PER SERVING)

Calories	218	
Total Fat	5.2g	7%
Saturated Fat	3.3g	16%
Cholesterol	0mg	0%
Sodium	3mg	0%
Total Carbohydrate	45.7g	17%
Dietary Fiber	7.7g	27%
Total Sugars	25.2g	
Protein	2.7g	

Tips: Fruits add their own natural sweetness, so use a balance of sweet and citrus fruits and reduce or eliminate other sweeteners like honey or maple syrup.

Spinach & Chervil Smoothie

| Prep time: 5 min | Cook time: 0 min | Servings: 2 |

Ingredients

- 2 cups spinach
- 1 cup chervil
- 1 cup mixed berries
- 2 oranges
- 2 limes
- 2 avocados
- 1 tbsp chia seed

Instructions

- Put all ingredients into a blender.

- Blend until smooth.
- Serve and enjoy!

NUTRITION FACTS (PER SERVING)

Calories	615	
Total Fat	41.6g	53%
Saturated Fat	8.4g	42%
Cholesterol	0mg	0%
Sodium	50mg	2%
Total Carbohydrate	64.1g	23%
Dietary Fiber	25.8g	92%
Total Sugars	24.5g	
Protein	11.3g	

Tips: Spinach, Chervil, and chia seeds are packed with iron. On the other hand, oranges, berries, avocados and limes contain a lot of vitamin C, which can increase the absorption of iron.

Ginger Turmeric Orange Juice

Prep time: 10 min	Cook time: 0 min	Servings: 4

Ingredients

- 2 apples, peeled and chopped
- 4 oranges, peeled
- 1 lemon, peeled
- 1 tbsp fresh ginger, minced
- 1 tbsp fresh turmeric, minced
- 2 cups water

Instructions

- Put the apples, oranges and lemon in a blender and mix until smooth.

- Add the ginger and turmeric and give it another boost.
- Pour in the water and squeeze until you get a smooth juice.
- Add more water for a milder juice.
- Serve and enjoy!

NUTRITION FACTS (PER SERVING)

Calories	159	
Total Fat	0.7g	1%
Saturated Fat	0.1g	1%
Cholesterol	0mg	0%
Sodium	6mg	0%
Total Carbohydrate	40.4g	15%
Dietary Fiber	8.1g	29%
Total Sugars	29.3g	
Protein	2.4g	

Tips: Studies suggest 500–2,000 mg of turmeric per day has potential benefits. Turmeric in extract form performs the best.

2-WEEK MEAL PLAN

1st Week Meal Plan

Day	Breakfast	Snack	Lunch	Dinner	Dessert
1	Devilled Eggs	Green Keto Smoothie	Thai Coconut Broccoli	Roasted Spiced Cauliflower	Sweet Carrot Cake
2	Chia Pudding	Honey Roasted Walnuts	Fried Rice	Eggs and Zoodles	Granola
3	Eggs with Asparagus	Super Food Smoothie	Spicy Chicken Stew	Healthy Carrot Fries	Nut Cups
4	Granola	Cabbage Chips	Broccoli Tabbouleh	Roasted Red Pepper Tomato Soup	Chia Smoothie
5	Shakshuka	Porridge	Turkey Fajita Bowl	Healthy Carrot Fries	Beet Brownies
6	Mushroom Omelet	Cocoa Balls	Baked Salmon	Zucchini Pasta Salad	Matcha Chai Pudding
7	Turkey Stuffed Avocado	Chia Smoothie	Pumpkin Soup	Sautéed Spinach with Stuffed Mushrooms	Blueberry Muffins

2nd Week Meal Plan

Day	Breakfast	Snack	Lunch	Dinner	Dessert
1	Vegetable Frittata	Super Food Smoothie	Crispy Sweet Potato Latkes	Zucchini Pasta Salad	Honey Roasted Walnuts
2	Granola	Green Keto Smoothie	Pumpkin Soup	Sautéed Spinach with Stuffed Mushrooms	Apple Cinnamon Granola Bars
3	Eggs with Asparagus	Chia Pudding	Spicy Chicken Stew	Cabbage Chips	Matcha Chai Pudding
4	Mushroom Omelet	Ginger Turmeric Orange Juice	Tofu Lettuce Wraps with Peanut Sauce	Roasted Spiced Cauliflower	Raspberry Muffin Energy Balls
5	Turkey Stuffed Avocado	Honey Roasted Walnuts	Baked Salmon	Roasted Red Pepper Tomato Soup	Pomegranate Smoothie
6	Chia Pudding	Pomegranate Smoothie	Broccoli Tabbouleh	Eggs and Zoodles	Cocoa Balls
7	Scrambled Eggs	Mint and Citrus Drink	Turkey Fajita Bowl	Healthy Carrot Fries	Sweet Carrot Cake